A magic brew

Andrea Hamilton

Presentation by *BookLeaf Publishing*

Web: www.bookleafpub.com

E-mail: info@bookleafpub.com

ISBN: 9789357214797

First edition 2022

To my daughter Sammie.

*To Jeanne and Wayne my beloved mother
and brother who I miss every day.*

*Both were my inspiration to life and writing
& art.*

ACKNOWLEDGEMENT

To my darling daughter, my wonderful grandson George and my best friend Lori.
To my sister Amber, her children, Kerri, Cogan and Brent.
And to everyone I have known and met.

.

PREFACE

A leaf fell, a petal danced.
I collected both, quite entranced.
I made some coffee, fresh and strong
Then dipped my foraged finds.
Pressed between the pages of an author's mind.

My Dress

I wore a dress everyday
It was not through poverty or cost
Nor laziness, nor illness
I was still and momentarily lost

The doors were locked
Yet my mind was not
The world had stilled you see
Through illness, confusion and loss
Dead inside, I did not much care a lot.

You see, I found time
Or was it, that it found me
Together we formed a plan
Daily rituals became as one
Time, my dress and me.

My dress became my inner self
I wore my insides out
Stripped bare of needing
I found I needed less.
The more I thought, the less came out.

My dress became a cloak
Of invisibility I dreamed

Ghostlike I roamed
An armor of fabric held fast against the world
My imagination perhaps was not all it seemed.

I fell in love with my dress
It anchored me to myself.
I felt safe, a friend, an acquaintance of old
And as I crept out from behind my facade
My dress, I kept, a reminder of my true self.

Elevated Grace

Elevated grace

What if Mary ran away to join the circus?
If her and Jesus ran –
Crossing seas, discovering places new.
If he held her hand –
Bloodied by rusting, cruelly driven nails.
They ran.
As stowaways –
Hiding under the canvas of night.
Joining the Travellers –
No need for questions.
A safe bed assured.
Mary learnt how to fly –
A bird of the heavens.
Jesus learnt how to throw –
Knives of Damascus steel.
She stitched sequins of celestial stars to her
costume –
He threw with bandaged hands.
She glinted as far away stars –
Falling from ropes of gold.
He crucified her upon a wheel –
Of red and white stripes.
She spun with grace and daring –

He never missed.
She danced with sawdust upon her feet –
Tulle skirts covering her modesty.
Fragile wings, clipped yet free –
Bread broken in friendship.
A caravan they shared –
Children they bared.
His father would have been happy –
Angels watched them from afar.
They wanted for nothing –
As nothing is free.

The stars

I stand by the shore, at the death of day.
A door opens-
The twilight sea calls-
For me to walk through.
to where I do not know.
As I stand by the shore
At the birth of night-
The silence is louder, the pitch more intense.
The universe hangs, as heavy velvet,
Soft, yet final and somewhat dense.
I walk into the darkness-
The lights come on-
Stars lit by an unknown hand.
Such beauty, such knowledge,
It tires my soul and so I shall sleep now-
My head lays upon moon moths and shredded
silks.
My eyelids covered in Shimmering dust.
Pray, a little, sing a little, perhaps a tear or two if
you must.
Remember me, for as I sail in perpetuity
Guided by the stars and the moon.
I shall leave a trail of magic sparkles,
So that I may return one day soon.

A 1000 days in Solitude

A 1ooo days in solitude.
Julian Assange
To the Max.
Maximum security
Unjustified, injustices –
Lawfare
Punishment by process
The American dream –
A dog with a bomb.
Ticking, the waiting game, chess for insurgents.
An opening gambit, Profit before lives
Banging at the door, bars, and corruption.
The truth is out there –
Who will believe, who will read the news, who cares?
Court hearings of lies and untruths.
Extradite, extradition, extinction –
Bars of confinement –
Belmarsh, the new Guantanamo.
Lockdown, Covid, isolation -
Do the right thing –
Scientific journalism, facts and truths.
Wiki Leaks reveals all –
Intelligent armies, analyse this, primary sources.

Iraq, Afghanistan, not on our doorstep, drone
away boys –
Who gives a fuck?
Everyone's a fucking Terrorist.
Except we do, we want the truth, we care about
the innocents.
The women and children, the maimed and
beaten –
Crucified by gods of stars and stripes.
Julian Assange cared –
He showed exceptional courage in the pursuit of
human rights –
Yet he languishes in jail, condemned, by our
own weak government.
Are they afraid of the truth?
Are they afraid of America?
Rubber stamp, extradite –
But wait what happens when the journalists are
no more –
Relics of a past, rewritten by time, move on
boys.
When the horses have bolted and the pigs rule -
With corruption and deceit.
Will we then listen, too late –
we shall live in ignorance.
Listening and believing what we are told –
No questions, no need, its all true now, isn't it –
Just take your joy mate and it will all be alright.

Dreaming of Death

The anchor has lifted
I am drifting.
Swept along by the currents as above and so
below.
I try to swim, but my arms are heavy
Weighted as the anchor that once bound.
I float, suspended in nothing, weightless, lost
and cold.
Does anyone care.
I begin to fall, sinking to soft sand, crustaceans
and grit.
Shrouded in the ocean's debris.
When the sands shift, will you find my bones?
I dance in the ebb and flow,
With grace, angelic and at peace.
Till a passing mermaid takes my hand.
A memento mori, a friend.
I smile, I laugh, oh how I laugh.
I give chase, it feels good, swimming against the
tides.
Exhilarated my breath short from the exertion.
I will not give up, I want my hand back!
Alive, alive o.

The vanishing land Whales

It is said that they once ruled the earth.
They're presence one of such magnitude.
We can barely fathom.
We stared in awe at their beauty.
They did not move
They could not move
But did they need to?
We honoured them as gods
They gave us with seas of plenty,
air of sweetness
and waters of blessings.
In time though, we forgot them, we left them to
die.
We did not give them gifts; we did not care.
They said it was the way of mankind to forget,
to discard.
Will we ever learn.
Yet perhaps it is not too late.
The gods have gone, buried deep in the earth,
but one day they shall return.
If we wished hard enough, we might catch a
glimpse.
Following our ancestors' path
Read their writings
Face their fears.

Our shame.
I wish I could go back to the old days,
to see the whales.
To say I am sorry.
Sorry my species is lost and that we do care.
It is our arrogance that kills, the innocent.

Flowerpots

Standing to attention atop the Aga.
Crusts risen to perfection –
Queens guards at the palace.
Browned to perfection.
Aromas of the finest perfumes –
Drift around the kitchen.
Freshly baked -
Hot to the touch, in there stone pots.
Waiting-
Tea towels swaddled them carefully –
picked up, as little babies.
Pop them out and watch them roll.
We laugh together.
My mother catches one-
She cuts with a surgeon's skill.
Soft dough -
Doorstep slices.
I spread two with creamy butter.
Savouring each bite, as it melts in your mouth.
A moment with mother-
In the heat of the kitchen, beside the Aga.
Dogs and cats spread before us as rugs on the
flagstone floor.

Menhir in an apron

They all talk about climate change –
Weathering storms and end of days, the
apocalypse and forebodings.
I get that –
I have weathered many.
I stand, a fossil of something I once was –
A Celtic beauty, strong lithe limbs, long dark
hair and deep flirtatious eyes.
I was swept up in the net of life, by a sailor boy
–

Then came marriage, and children.
Now, I stand beauty decayed and long worn
down.
My brow furrowed, lines so deep, ploughed by
an unknown hand –
Tattoos of time etched around my eyes-
Drawn by life itself.
I stand, a standing stone, a Menhir in an apron.
Domesticated, chained to a sink, forever stating
through the small windowpane.
When my Sailor man died, my apron remained.
I wear it still, as a medal, a memento, a comfort
–

Memories of my children's lifespans are marked
into the cloth.

They flew the nest long ago, taking some threads
to start new nests.
Nothing has changed, though a little quieter now
–

Standing is an art form, like the Mona Lisa with
her perpetual smile-
Staring at nothing, yet searching for something.
I have marked my time here well.
This fossil is growing legs again, or perhaps a
tail –
She will learn to walk again, or to swim in the
wild seas.
One step at a time, they say –
As I open the door to freedom –
To deal myself back in.
The sea beckons, salt fresh upon my face,
seagulls wishing me luck.
 I shall stand no more, I have done my duty.

The Cornish stone maiden

She stands, a loney figure, staring towards the sea, a sentry of Kemite, her forlorn outline leaning with grace, awaiting the setting sun of each day. Ever since she can remember, she has stood, the sea her companion. She knows not why she stands, for her memory tires of trying, the years have passed as the clouds overhead. She has few comforts, the ebb and flow of the sea and the gulls that circle ceaslessly above her head, piercing the air with their haunting cries. Far out to sea, upon the rocks, named by cornish verse, sit the Mermaids, singing as the gulls with piercing beauty. They laugh, with each other, with the oceans swells, oh sometimes how sweet, lingering upon the air, as perfume, notes of poigancy upon the breeze.

She wishes she could laugh too, but she is made of stone, yet once when the earth was ruled by magic, she too could sing. But that was long long ago, she cannot remember why she stopped.

There is still magic she tells herself, when the sun, lulls the sea to sleep, stiling his surface as a mirror, reflecting a thousand smiles. She feels alive again, her quartz fragments sparkling as diamonds, bathed in the Cornish light.

A robin sits close by, his tiny dark eyes, twinkle with a steely glint, a brave soldier in a red waistcoat, alert and bright resting for but a brief moment. The downey grey of his feathers, looks so soft, she wonders what it would be like to sleep on a bed of feathers, would they be softer than grass she wonders.

At her feet grows samphire, succulent snd sweet, with scattered sea pinks, adding a blaze of colour, delicately fanned by the lacey branches of a Tamarisk tree. Sea spume is carried upon the winds breath, blowing salty kisses upon the stone maidens face, wetting the lichen that grows on her cheeks.

On occaision a traveller passes by, touching her cold stone or perhaps resting by her side. She like to hear their tales, of far away places and mortal woes and sometimes even a wish is made.

And when winter come around, whipping the sea into a frenzy of madness, she prays for the ships to pass by safely, for too many have been lost, smashed upon the carreg rocks, the sailrs cries mixed with the gulls, taken by nature and wreckers. She shivers inside, for those poor lost souls condemned to die, clinging onto fragments of their mortal lives.

Oh how she would weep for them.
And so she stands, a Menhir for all to see to the
end of time.

A Witch I shall be –

Why does everyone want to be a witch, and can
I be one too?

Forget princesses and fairies – how boring.

Though, fairies bite and kick ass, so I am told.

No, I want black, long and flowing,

A stream of allure in obsidian darkness.

Silver rings that sparkle and glint, as a crow's
eye.

I want to be powerful, know thyself they say.

I want to feel part of a secret society,

The unknown women's society.

With quiet knowing's, a sly look, and a wink.

Freemasons of women, for women.

I want to run free, hellishly dancing as I choose.

No restraints, no constraints, no, no, no.

I want a hat, pointy and tall, that warns of danger.

Shadowing my face in mystery, as a widow's veil might.

Pointy shoes, ever so dainty with Victorian heels,

Clicking upon marble floors, with an air of authority.

I want a black cat, that purrs in my ear,

A familiar comfort, watching with feigned interest.

Tarot cards to shuffle,

 held in my hands, as a devilish spread.

And a wand to wave, as a sword in battle,

Made by a Gypsy for a silver charm.

I'll need a Grimoire, all witches do,

I shall write spells in oak gall ink,

And draw Sigils from angel's wings,

I'm sure they won't miss a feather or two.

So, mote it be, is what I shall say,

Three times a day,

A witch I shall be

A Witch I shall be

A witch I shall be

.

Disillusioned

On the other side of the tracks.

There's no grass, but dirt,

Dry as bones.

Powdered by the hands of God –

Strewn around as the wind takes its fancy.

In your face, your eyes –

sitting upon parched skin, impossible to remove.

An unwelcome visitor –

ingrained, as memories.

Forged memories, deep and unforgiving.

Streaks upon white skin-

Scars, tattoos, reminders.

Drifters, bums, is this is life-

Then I lost.

The turn of a dice, a game of cards -.

 wife, kids, all long gone.

So, I drift, like prairie grass, carried upon the
wind -.

Winds of fate, I chose mine.

Bourbon lips, sharp rocks, cut you deep-

I raise my hand.

One for the road barman-

I'll be on my way.

Soon I'll be dust, in the company of worms-

Perhaps the sting of a scorpion-

to remind me of life.

As the lone Indian walking to death-

I go alone.

You never knew me-

never will, but I know myself.

A lost cowboy's footsteps leaving trails in the
dust-

My Mustang drives me forward.

A dream of long ago-

As the wind blows them all away and the
landscape takes me home.

Adieu.

To Forage

We forage through the discarded
The bins of waste, temples of salvation
Sifting through the debris of others.
Thrown into the daily tides of unrelenting
consumerism.
Food to eat.
Necessity.

Overspill from factories.
End of rolls, end of life, raw selvedge.
Imperfect, mass produced, mass fodder.
Endless stitching, slave labour, endless poverty.
We relish the new.
Consumer foraging, retail shops.
Amazon, Internet.
It matters not where
As long as it's new, unworn, untouched by a
body.

Titt for Tatt, discarded tatt.
Given freely, sold at a price
Rag and bone, gone to the dogs
Shabby chic is the new old.
Blots on the landscape, fly tipping.
Remains of the old.

I forage in nature's own garden; she does not
mind.
Plants to heal, scars to hide.
Natures not picky, she gives freely.
Weeds give life, hope, where there is none.

Will my art live on when I am gone?
Recycled, a patchwork quilt, laid to rest
A shroud of scraps
Graffiti upon discarded buildings
Books torn and burnt
Ashes flying upwards as charred stars
Back to the earth
Landfill
Another's treasures.

Torn

Pulled apart by love
Destroyed by pain.
A hurt so deep.
Cuts inflicted by others
Scars deep within.
Betrayed by your own flesh-
A child of your body.
Torn from you.
As flesh from a bone-
Your bones.
Stripped bare –
Naked.
Tears falling –
Salty streaks against reddened cheeks.
A river, never stopping –
They cannot, you cannot.
You are a stranger –
A stranger to yourself.
A shadow of what was -
Cast aside.
Upon tides of fate.
Alone you stand –
An empty shell,
Upon an endless beach.

The storm in a Teacup

The storm rises, the signs are there, the
warnings.
The swell as the tide turns.
We see only what we want to.
Until the rain lashes down with our tears do we
find the clues.
We pick at the evidence –
As crows on the bones.
We question ourselves –
We blame ourselves.
The if only creeps in –
Insidious as a ghost, a traitor to our memories.
We start to make plans –
We must.
But what did they like –
Can you remember, was they're a will?
Paperwork, overwhelms, the enormity threatens
to drown us.
We are lost at sea-
 Floating, drifting, nothing makes sense
anymore.
Life is so fragile –
Paper cut outs, dissolving in water.
A service booklet –
Words and images, memento mori.

A shrine to the lost –
Photos treasured and candles burned.
Windows of Sea glass –
I peer through to your soul.
Oh, my dear departed –
Time will heal they say.
Yet time is no keeper –
If we wait, we wait forever –
It cannot be bottled; it cannot be tied with
threads.
It must be released, set free to the winds–
For only then can time heal.
Farewell my friend –
We shall meet again soon –
When the stars align and the ladder is thrown
down.
I shall climb to heavens path –
Guided by the stars –
With an old broken compass and a broken heart.

After Sylvia Plath

Dear, dear Sylvia,
May I ask, why?
She simply smiled, her beautiful face, blank –
"I don't know what made me do it –
I can't say I was coerced.
The children were playing quietly in the other
room.
I was making a cup of tea –
Staring out from the window.
Thinking how still the day –
 I could have been sleepwalking, not really
aware.
The air felt calm, a thin veil of tranquillity –
Across my face, as if, already dead.
A widow at the graveside, looking at myself.
I remember thinking, how nice it would be to
sleep forever.
I could hear the birds singing, their shrill sounds
pierced the air.
My breathing had become slow, yet my heart,
beat heavy upon my chest,
Flooding my ears with rhythmic drumbeats –
My body wanted to dance, but my feet would
not move, or couldn't perhaps.

I felt as a ghost, not here nor there, just
somewhere , how odd.
My beloved children were playing in the room
next door.
A memory.
Or my memory playing with me -
My books, my writings, lay scattered about -
How quietly they play, so peaceful.
I know they must be missing me –
I miss them dreadfully.
The kitchen is at least tidy –
Someone has cleaned up; did I leave a mess?
I don't believe so –
Ted would be very cross –
He abhorred mess.
He will miss me, will he cry?
I feel as a paper doll, cut out from the pages of
his writings.
Such, prowess, a great man, yet I still stand in
his shadow, as a ghost.
 I am fading now, yet, I still can't answer your
question.
But its nice here, they look after me and my
fragile ego.
I shall write, I promise.
Look, she blew on the glass of a mirror.
Ghostly letters appeared upon the glass, quite
naughty, but delightful fun.
I feel so young again.

I guess life is there for the living.
How quietly they play, so peaceful.
Did you read my book, I poured my soul into it.
As water to a vase.
"I, loved it", I reply, "as did so very many, you
were so talented and sorely missed"
She smiles.
The vase of flowers looks so beautiful.

The American Dream - To Hiati

"Round em up cowboy"
Rein them in, lashes, no guns.
Roll up, Roll up
For the greatest show on earth-
Media clash, fake news, death of the journalist.
Oh how you stole the show-
And a few countries too.
Histories of blood-
Founded by father's unknown.
Washed hands in streams of tears-
Relish your riches in jars of preserves.

"Pack em in boys"
Remember the old days-
Planes now, not ships.
Mass expulsions, no chains required-
Poste haste, back to black.
I killed a man in Rio-
Not on our doorstep.

"Old Hiati"
Gracious queen of resilience-
Revered by all, a calling card.
Voodou, mystery, Kompa-

Dances with angels and demons.
Feathers and crosses, floods, and tears.
Les etoiles-
The stars mourn and weep.
"American corruption"
2nd class, no class-
Caste out.
Despised because of poverty,
Yet they keep you in poverty.
Cages made of barbed wire-
Stars and stripes of bondage.
I pray to Marie Laveau-
That you stand strong and proud again-
Overlapping in crisis, dignity, and grace.
Chart a course-
Through turbulent seas,
Freedom to choose, new leaders.
To choose life.

The Door to my wild self

I found some magic in a book
The door to my wild self, is within my reach
I found the key inside a jar
All rusty and old
Weathered as iron upon a beach

The lock was hidden, inside an old oak tree
Covered in Ivy, knurled by time, so very old
It fitted well, but wouldn't turn
I tried each day and night
Till exhausted and my fingers cold.

Each day I took a turn, my intention was true
Each day I failed.
I cried, and to myself I did scold
I made a wish, I said a prayer
I begged, please let me through.

I stood and said, I must seek my path and be
bold
And so it turned
Slowly at first
Creaking with the resentment of age
A crack of light appeared and I walked through
that door
To discover my wild self of old.

The American Insurgence

So you pulled out-
The American Insurgence.
The rape of a nation.
Hey Joe-
Look across the tracks.
Cashmere covered warfare,
Drones threaded high.
Shadows of contempt,
Cover your sins.
Shrouds of death,
Hidden in the dust and valleys.
Guns laid down, but no truce.
You simply walked.
Deserted, people abandoned.
Bin Laden murdered-
Cold blooded.
People have pride, dignity.
Yet falseness and lies are the new deal.
A pack of cards.
The game is not over.
Merely left for the innocents to pick up the
pieces.
To selvedge from the ashes of nothing.
The Americans punish withholding funds-
From a pillaged country.

They deserve better.
Shame upon a mighty nation-
who steals with corruption-
Black oil runs deep in your veins.
Familiarity of wealth breeds Contempt for others
poverty.
A graveyard quilt to cover your sins.

Tread softly upon my carpet
—

Tread softly upon my carpet –
Laid,
to honour of the oaken king.
Before he bows out to the winters Crone.
Fallen leaves layered as feathers –
Tablecloths Laid out in celebration -
For the feasts to come.
Colours that speak of rejoicement -
Alchemists' golds, bloodied reds, purples of
royalty.
Greens and browns of the earth -
autumnal splendours-
strewn with great abandonment –
A celebration of heavenly magnitude.
The yearly event, never to be missed -
The trees whisper coyly, as maids in a row.
Rustling with laughter as their Confetti leaves
fall -
The wind blows orchestral octaves,
through the lace gloves of branches.
Ladies, waving, to all, join the dance.
Dance with us, dance, dance till you can no
more.
 Ancestors and ghosts of the past –

To everyone alive, rejoice, join me in the dance.
Dance as you forage before the savageness of
winter bites –
Dance with grace in the dimming nights.
Dance with flickering candles shing in the dark.
 Pumpkins glowing, eyes watching.
Raise a glass of cider mulled -
Wear the darkness as a cloak.
A red ribbon tied around a tree.
A neckerchief of gypsy's magic.
Dance, we shall, to autumns death –
And the winters graveyard.
Of ice and frost.

Torn - As paper

Torn
Not clean
As a pressed shirt
Or sharp as a crisp prosecco
Sharp folds of pressed sheets
No jagged edges
Friendship intact
Crisp white cartridge paper

Torn
As jagged crevices
Deep and unknown
Falling
Out of control
Cuts, gashes, bruises
Hard knocks
Pumice stones, volcanic eruptions.
Lava and pain spilled
Blotting paper, to blot the tears.

Torn
Venomous words
poison
Burnt paper, third degree burns
Broken bodies and minds

Lies tearing apart
Justified actions
Rag paper, strong in defence.

Torn
Paper ripped from a page
Crumpled into a ball
By hands of anger
Tossed
A salad of words unkind
Caged in the waste.

Torn
Bloodied on the floor
Bones broken
Dark bruises of defeat
Fear
Verbal violence
The shouting
fly little bird fly
Rag paper torn to make wings.

Memento Mori

Her graceful fingers, held no fear.
They cut the skin, cold and dead.
His eyes stared to the heavens.
A dead mans eyes can weep no tears.

Yet she shed her tears, for no mortal could she
keep.
The ocean ebbed and flowed, Mourning with
loss.
The gulls cried.
And all around could only weep.

Piece by piece the flesh was removed.
Mankind's fabric inked with life.
Images and words, poetry
Stolen forever.

A sweetheart's loss, a mothers pain.
She cuts with grace and stitched with tenderness.
Tokens to keep.
Never shall his sweet voice sing again.

In grief, she sang, words lost to time.
A magic so old, even the Angels heard.
They took his soul, to the realms above.

She closed his eyes, with a stitch
And a gold coin pressed tight.

His tattoos were neatly sewn and patched upon
her tail.
An anchor, a swallow, names of love.
Patchwork of faded memories.